Parenting Children with Oppositional Defiant Disorder for Beginners

A Modern, Comprehensive, and Practical O.D.D. Guide to Understand and Help Your Child with Powerful and Simple Techniques (7 Step Parenting Plan)

Olivia Harris

Legal Notice:
Copyright 2022 by Olivia Harris - All rights reserved.

This document is geared towards providing exact and reliable information regarding the topic and issue covered. The publication is sold on the idea that the publisher is not required to render an accounting, officially permitted, or otherwise, qualified services. If advice is necessary, legal or professional, a practiced individual in the profession should be ordered.
From a Declaration of Principles which was accepted and approved equally by a Committee of the American Bar Association and a Committee of Publishers and Associations.

Legal Notes:
In no way is it legal to reproduce, duplicate, or transmit any part of this document by either electronic means or in printed format. Recording of this publication is strictly prohibited and any storage of this document is not allowed unless with written permission from the publisher. All rights reserved.
The information provided herein is stated to be truthful and consistent, in that any liability, in terms of inattention or otherwise, by any usage or abuse of any policies, processes, or directions contained within is the solitary and utter responsibility of the recipient reader. Under no circumstances will any legal responsibility or blame be held against the publisher for any reparation, damages, or monetary loss due to the information herein, either directly or indirectly. Respective authors own all copyrights not held by the publisher.

Disclaimer Notice:
The information herein is offered for informational purposes solely and is universal as so. The presentation of the information is without a contract or any type of guarantee assurance. Readers acknowledge that the author is not engaging in the rendering of legal, financial, medical or professional advice. Please consult a licensed professional before attempting any techniques outlined in this book.
By continuing with this book, readers agree that the author is under no circumstances responsible for any losses, indirect or direct, that are incurred as a result of the information presented in this document, including, but not limited to inaccuracies, omissions and errors.

The trademarks that are used are without any consent, and the publication of the trademark is without permission or backing by the trademark owner. All trademarks and brands within this book are for clarifying purposes only and are the owned by the owners themselves, not affiliated with this document.

Table of Contents

The Fundamentals of the Oppositional Defiant Disorder 4

The Latest Scientific Research 10

Powerful, Simple, and Efficient 7 Step Parenting Plan to Help Your Child Improve 16

Create a Custom Behaviour Plan for Your Child 39

The Psychology of Child's Defiance and How to Deal with it in a Quick and Efficient Manner 52

Dangers and Mistakes You Must Avoid 61

How to Build Your Child's Self-Esteem 68

Teaching Your Child Skills for Everyday Life 73

How to Help Your Child with Friendships and Socialising 79

Breathing Techniques and Suggestions for Handling Intense Emotions 86

Path to Outgrowing O.D.D. 93

How to Monitor Child's Behaviour Progress and Improve it with Behaviour Mapping 96

Conclusion 101

The Fundamentals of the Oppositional Defiant Disorder

If you have a child who has recently been diagnosed with Oppositional Defiant Disorder (O.D.D.), or if you're awaiting a diagnosis and wanting to learn and understand more about this condition, this book is for you. We are going to cover everything you need to know about O.D.D., including the basics of this condition, the latest research, parenting tips, mistakes to avoid, and more. With this information, you should be well-positioned to help your child deal with this disorder and function as well as possible. This is not an easy condition to handle, but this book will give you the tools you need to be an effective, compassionate, caring parent that is capable of helping your child cope.

One of the important things to remember when you start dealing with this kind of diagnosis is that you are not alone. There are many parents out there that are grappling with this kind of challenging behaviour, doubting their abilities, and feeling at the end of their tether. With time, you will master the techniques that should make the behaviour easier to handle, but bear in mind that the most important thing is to be kind and patient with both your child and yourself. It will make life much easier for you if you recognise that you are both trying your best.

With that said, let's start looking at the fundamentals of O.D.D. and what you can expect to see if your child has this condition. This is a behavioural disorder that needs to be diagnosed by a medical professional, and it can overlap with other conditions, but it is recognised as its own unique disorder. If you think that your child may have O.D.D. and you have not yet sought help, get in touch with local healthcare professionals, as it is a condition that puts a lot of pressure on the family and on the child. With help from experts, you should be able to master it.

Commonest Signs Of O.D.D.:

Before we start, it's worth noting that a lot of the symptoms that are commonly associated with O.D.D. are also seen in children and teenagers without O.D.D. They are especially prevalent when those children are tired, upset, hungry, or otherwise frustrated. However, these symptoms are much more likely to be seen in children with O.D.D., and they are much more strongly expressed than in other children.

They may not be linked with low mood or have clear causes, and you might see them on a very regular basis, and to extreme degrees. These symptoms tend to include:

1) Deliberate attempts to provoke a negative reaction from people nearby (e.g. annoy or upset those people). Note that the behaviour must be intentional and aimed at causing frustration.
2) Getting annoyed or upset very easily, showing touchy behaviour and sensitivity even when the provocation is minor.
3) Interest in revenge and a spiteful attitude towards other people, especially when upset by something.

4) Aggressive speech when something has caused upset, including angry language and obvious resentment.

5) Regular temper tantrums that may last for a long time.

6) Questioning of rules and reluctance to follow them.

7) Regular and excessive arguing, especially with adults in a position of authority.

8) Disobedience and a refusal to follow requests to do or not do something.

9) Reluctance to take responsibility for mistakes; children with O.D.D. will often blame something that they have done on others.

All of these behaviours are negative and can create a lot of hostility between the child and those around them, especially their caregivers, who are the ones most likely to be setting rules, making requests, and handling the child. These caregivers may become frequent targets for the child's attempts to provoke a negative response, because they are often the focus of the child's attention. However, children with O.D.D. may also try to get this sort of response from other children that they are interacting with, or from other adults. The behaviour can make it extremely difficult for the child to interact well with peers, which will prevent them from forming strong social bonds with anyone, especially children their own age, who may not be able to make allowances the way that adults can. This can cause all kinds of problems and is very frustrating for the child's caregivers. It may also leave the child feeling lonely, depressed, and isolated, which can contribute to other mental disorders and problems, and needs to be dealt with as soon as possible. If you are looking after a child who suffers from O.D.D., you should seek support from health organisations local to you. It is critical that you and your child both receive a good degree of support, as you are likely to face major challenges while parenting your child, and you will need tactics and techniques that are effective. We will explore many in this book, but it will still be beneficial to have someone working with you and determining your child's specific needs.

In some cases, O.D.D. can be partially treated using medication, but you will also be taught how to deal with your child's behaviour in effective, productive ways. You will probably do some "parent training," as well as collaborative problem solving, and multisystemic therapy. Your child may attend peer group therapy to improve their interpersonal skills, and family therapy to improve communication and build relationships among all family members, including siblings – who often suffer when their brother or sister has O.D.D. Cognitive behavioural therapy is another common treatment.

Often, all caregivers for the child – including teachers – will be involved in some of the treatment processes so that they will have the tools to deal with the child's behaviour when it becomes difficult. This tends to be a more effective way of dealing with O.D.D. than the child attending therapy alone. In general, both the caregivers and the child need to make changes to their behaviour; just leaving it up to your child will not be enough to resolve the issues that the child is facing.

The Latest Scientific Research

The science surrounding O.D.D. is constantly being updated as scientists do further studies on what causes and exacerbates the symptoms of O.D.D., so it's important to check in with your doctor for any updated information – but for now, let's look at where the research has got to.

What Causes O.D.D.?

There are no known causes for O.D.D., and there is still a lot of dispute about this condition and what factors may contribute to its development. However, it has been heavily linked with both ADHD and Autism, and it is thought that only around 10 per cent of children who do not suffer from one of these two conditions will suffer from O.D.D.

There is thought to be a genetic component, but a great deal more study is needed to pinpoint why and how O.D.D. develops. Until we understand more, it isn't safe to state that O.D.D. is caused by either genetic or environmental factors, but it is likely that both play a role. However, the current research indicates that the heritability of O.D.D. is around 50 per cent.[i] There is also thought to be a link with children who have been exposed to abuse, and children who have been given inconsistent teachings and rules. Other issues with instability, such as poverty, neighbourhood violence, peer rejection, and more could contribute to the development of O.D.D. It is therefore quite likely that both the environment and the genetics are significant when dealing with O.D.D.

It is also worth noting that O.D.D. is more commonly seen among males than females in the younger ages, but this disparity could be due to under-diagnosis among females, rather than due to more males having O.D.D. The disparity disappears as the children get older, with an equal number of diagnoses in teenage males and females.

When Does O.D.D. Develop?

O.D.D. can be diagnosed at any stage of a person's life, but some children can be diagnosed as young as pre-school: tests may be done once a child has turned 5 years old. Of course, not all defiant behaviour is an indication that your child has O.D.D.: it is perfectly normal for children to challenge and defy authority figures as part of growing up, testing boundaries, and expanding their confidence. It is only when this is taken to the extremes that children tend to be tested for O.D.D.

There are various tests that can be used to diagnose O.D.D., and these include:

- The Child and Adolescent Psychiatric Assessment
- The Child Behaviour Checklist
- The Disruptive Behaviour Diagnostic Observation Schedule
- The Conners Child Behaviour Checklist
- The Behaviour Assessment for Children
- The Development and Well-Being Assessment
- The Strength and Difficulties Questionnaire

It is important that other tests are done to determine whether there are other factors at play, including learning disabilities. Risk factors such as bullying, anxiety disorders, OCD, and more should also be considered. The medical professional may assess the child alongside their friends, teachers, siblings, parents, and more, so that they can see how the child responds to different inputs and scenarios. The idea is to build an overall picture of the child, assess all aspects of their growth, development, and interactions, and then draw an accurate assessment of their situation and conditions. This will help to determine whether your child has O.D.D. or other conditions.

Will My Child Grow Out Of O.D.D.?

There is some debate about this question, and it seems likely that some children do grow out of O.D.D., especially if they are given the necessary support and guidance. Others may just get better as they gradually develop coping strategies. However, many children who suffer from O.D.D. go on to develop other conditions, including depression, ADHD, anxiety, and more as they get older. This can result in criminal behaviour and a more serious diagnosis of conduct disorder. It is therefore very important to get your child the help that they need to overcome these issues, rather than ignoring them and hoping that your child will grow out of them.

Can O.D.D. Be Prevented?

Again, this question doesn't necessarily have a clear answer either way, but it does seem that O.D.D. can be prevented or made less severe through careful intervention, especially when the child is young. Even older children and teens can have the symptoms of O.D.D. lessened using certain techniques. Methods for young children may include things like talking therapy, learning better social skills, anger management, and more.

For teenagers, talking therapy, help with schoolwork, and practising social skills may help.

It is very important for the parent to be part of the process, and to learn techniques for themselves. Effective discipline, behaviour management, and positive reinforcement are all key aspects that a parent needs to cover if they are going to learn how to manage their child's behaviour, and if you are looking after a child with O.D.D., you must be prepared to spend time on each of these things. Without a caregiver who is well equipped to manage the challenges of O.D.D., the child is much more likely to struggle and suffer. You should make use of any support systems that are in place, but make sure you are learning how to deal with the behaviour, rather than just hoping your child's therapy will help them to overcome it.

Powerful, Simple, and Efficient 7 Step Parenting Plan to Help Your Child Improve

As a parent, you need to be able to control your child's behaviour and moods to some degree, and that might feel impossible when you're dealing with a child who suffers from O.D.D. – but it isn't. With the right techniques and skills, you can encourage your O.D.D. child to respond to you in ways that are more positive, and you will be able to set both yourself and your child up for success. Many of these techniques will take time to establish and turn into effective strategies, so you will need to persevere and keep working at them. Remember as you do that you and your child are a team, even if it doesn't feel like it, and together you are working to overcome something extremely challenging.

Be proud of each step that you take, even if it feels small and inconsequential in the face of the bigger problems. Be aware that you are the person your child looks to for guidance and affection when the world is frightening, and that even if your child is provoking you in every way possible, even when they say things that are hurtful and unkind, they love you and their world revolves around you. No matter how difficult your child is being, you need to aim for patience, kindness, and affection in all of your dealings with them.

You should also take the time to be kind to yourself and remember that you are grappling with immensely challenging behavioural problems, and that it is okay to mess up occasionally. You aren't going to get it right every time and that's perfectly acceptable. Don't be too hard on yourself on the days when you struggle to give your child everything they need; it is okay to make mistakes, as long as you are also learning and improving.

With that in mind, let's look at some strategies that you can use to help yourself and your child overcome some of the challenges associated with O.D.D. so that you can both enjoy life to the fullest. With these tools and techniques, as well as ones that you will be given by medical professionals, you should soon find that life with an O.D.D. child gets easier and less stressful – although you are still bound to experience challenges at times.

1) Have A Clearly Communicated Plan

There are two parts to this strategy: the first involves having a plan, and the second involves expressing it to your child. Some people may find that this comes more naturally to them than others, because some people are keen planners, while other people like to take life as it comes and only have a vague outline for each day.

Regardless of which strategy you generally favour, when it comes to raising a child with O.D.D., you should have a plan for every day.

If your child is a visual learner, you may want to write this down and share it with your child in a format that is clear and fixed. It can help to have some cornerstones for each day (e.g. dinner time at 6 PM, bath-time at 8 PM, etc.). Knowing what is going to happen makes it easier for a lot of children who have behavioural problems, because they aren't taken by surprise when something happens, and they can plan accordingly. You are much less likely to get a negative response to an instruction if they are prepared for the instruction in advance.

You should experiment with different planning strategies

and see which works best for you and your child. Some parents find that having an overall plan but just sharing the key steps or the next two events with their child works well. Some find that having a plan for the whole day and communicating this is the best method. This should then be followed up with regular reminders shortly before the change of an activity. For example, you might say to your child, "In half an hour, we are going to the park." You can keep offering these reminders as the time gets shorter, so there's no shock when the transition comes.

Even if your child is young, you can implement this sort of planning strategy. You will need to adapt it to your child's current reading ability, but if you're working with a very young child, you can use pictures to let them know about key events that are coming up. This will help them to anticipate things and get themselves ready, and increases the chances of a positive or at least reasonable response when the activity changes. Your child will also feel a greater sense of control over their own activities when you treat them in this way.

If you tell your child that you want them to stop playing and get into bed immediately, they are much less likely to respond well. They are engaged with play and have not even thought about bedtime. Remember that children live very much in the moment, so employing this sort of sudden stop to an activity can be jarring for them. Instead, you should approach this gently, so that they have time to make the transition and get their minds around the idea that a change is about to occur. This will probably look something like the following:

"It's bedtime in half an hour."

"It's bedtime in 20 minutes."

"It's bedtime in 10 minutes."

"It's bedtime in 5 minutes."

"It's bedtime in 2 minutes."

"It's bedtime now."

How many reminders you need will depend on your child, but this sort of approach tends to be very effective in improving their response, because it gives them a better sense of how to use their time and ensures they feel in control, rather than being caught out by a sudden change.

You may also want to use a visual timer so that your child has something they can watch and refer to when they want to know how long they have left. This can be very effective if you are busy, and it increases the sense of control for your child.

Even if your child can't tell the time yet, you can use this strategy. You simply need an analogue clock, and then you can tell your child something along the lines of, "When the big hand is on the 12 and the little hand is on the 8, it will be time to get into bed."

Combine these two approaches, and you are much more likely to have a willing child when bedtime comes. This can work with little children, but it's also possible to employ the same strategy for older children too. Consider getting your child their own watch and encouraging them to be responsible for paying attention to it. Talk to them about the plan for the day, give them a schedule, and encourage them to pay attention to it.

Make sure that you stick to the schedule as much as possible, especially once you have shared it with your child, as many children struggle when plans change suddenly, and feel overwhelmed or upset. Use an alarm if possible, and keep things predictable where you can. You can make your child more responsible for their own time awareness, but keep them involved in what you are going to do, why you are going to do it, and how it is going to unfold. This will really help.

You can adjust this strategy to suit your needs as a family, but it is one of the best that you can employ with children who suffer from O.D.D. How detailed your schedule is will depend on you and your child, but have at least a basic one that shows the important parts of the day (getting up and going to bed, mealtimes, trips out, bath-time, etc.).

2) Use Praise And Be Specific

You probably know the saying that you will catch more flies with honey than vinegar, and this has never been more true than when raising a child with behavioural challenges. If you get angry and frustrated and you let this show in your voice and behaviour, your child is going to pick up on the negativity and respond negatively too.

This doesn't mean that you can never scold your child or exert your authority, but remember that your day to day demeanour should be positive. This is the best way to build a good relationship with your child, and with a good relationship, you will enjoy more positive behaviour overall.

Positive reinforcement is therefore a valuable tool in your arsenal, and you should take every opportunity you get to use this with your child. Whenever they do something well, you should be prepared with praise – but it needs to be specific. An empty "That was good" will not mean much to your child and won't tell them what they should do in the future. "You picked your toys up very nicely," offers far more information that your child can use to shape their responses to a future request. They can learn what behaviour is desirable by listening to you praise them, and this is far more effective than listening to what behaviour isn't desirable.

This reinforces the behaviour because no child truly wants to be garnering negative attention all the time. By encouraging your child to do the things you want with positivity, rather than steering them away from the things you don't want with negativity, you'll also have a much easier time, because it's quicker to define what you want your child to do than to list all the things that you don't want them to do.

3) Offer Choices When You Can

Sometimes, as a parent, you need your child to do something even when they don't want to – and there's no second option. You can't ask them whether they want to eat dinner or not; they need to eat dinner. However, there is often scope for at least some choice in most of these situations, and giving them this may help to soften their behaviour at times. It can also give them a greater sense of control over the situation, and make them feel involved in the things that happen to them.

Examples of this might include things like asking whether they would like X or Y for dinner, or which set of pyjamas they would like to wear. You may find that your child responds better to two or three concrete choices, rather than an open ended "What would you like for dinner?" so make sure you try both strategies and determine which is the most effective for you.

For older children, you can make this strategy more complicated, but the basic premise remains the same.

By offering a choice related to the thing that you want them to do, you make it clear that the thing is going to happen, but that they do have some control over it and how it happens. Choices will often stop a fight before it starts, because they distract the child from whether they want to do something or not, and instead focus their attention on how they want to do it.

4) Use Positive Directions, Rather Than Negative Directions

When you tell your child to stop doing something, you are creating a negative association with your words and implicitly making the world worse by taking away an activity that they were enjoying. You also leave it open ended so that they can get into more trouble; they may stop doing that particular thing, but start doing something else problematic. This can lead to frustration for you as you try harder and harder to control your child by telling them to stop, stop stop, and your child will also get frustrated because they feel like everything they do results in criticism. Even if they are deliberately choosing activities to frustrate you, they will feel negative when they constantly hear you saying stop.

Instead, choose a positive framing for your words; this makes it much easier for a child to obey. For example, instead of saying "stop playing with your food," say "eat your dinner nicely." Your child will feel encouraged by the positive, and will have a clear instruction that they can much more easily follow.

You can do this with almost any instruction, and you should spend some time working out how to frame directives as positives, instead of negatives. You can see some examples below:

"Stop playing with your toys; it's time for bed." = "Come and get into bed."

"Stop splashing in the bath." = "Keep the water in the bath."

"Stop running." = "Walk nicely."

"Don't hit me." = "Treat me gently."

"Don't ignore me." = "Listen to me."

It may take some time to master this pattern of speaking, especially if you have slipped into quite a negative way of thinking lately; it isn't instinctive to choose positive framings when you are frustrated and annoyed by something. However, doing so will likely make you feel better as well as your child, because it puts the focus on what you want them to do, not what you want them to stop doing, and this can make the whole situation feel more constructive.

It's clearer and will result in a much more positive atmosphere overall, so use this to your advantage.

You might find that it helps to make yourself some cheat sheets, especially for areas that are particularly problematic with your child. Sometimes, it's hard to frame a negative instruction as a positive, but with a bit of creativity, you should find a way.

5) Be Empathetic

When you're busy being the figure of authority in your child's life, it can be very easy to forget to empathise with your child. This isn't because you don't care about them or because you are an unfeeling person. It's simply that you want a job doing and you want the result to be reached as efficiently as possible. When you're a busy, stressed, tired parent, it's easy to give an instruction and expect it to be followed, regardless of what your child thinks or feels about it. After all, you are the parent and your rules need to be followed for the household to function.

However, a bit of empathy can go a very long way. After all, your child is a person with their own wants and feelings, and they will be developing their own systems of logic – and sometimes, they aren't going to want to do something just because you have said that they should. It isn't always easy to rationalise with a young child, but you can still empathise with them.

Empathy is probably one of the best tools you have against O.D.D. because it proves to the child that you are on their side.

If they are starting to develop negative responses to figures of authority and feel frustrated by them, that's likely because they don't feel listened to or in control – and you can do something about the former of those at least.

You should therefore show that you know how they feel and that you respect and acknowledge those feelings – even if that doesn't change the facts. For example, you can say to your child, "I know you are feeling very frustrated by your homework right now. It is hard to do. You still need to do it, but it will be finished soon, and you're doing a great job."

You could say "I know you're angry because you can't have cake before dinner. It does feel like you should be allowed to. You can't have cake, but it's okay to be upset."

This demonstrates to the child that you understand their emotions and that those emotions are valid. Their homework still needs to be done, or they still can't have cake, but they are allowed to feel angry about it. You should also add some praise if they are handling it well.

This will encourage them and make them feel proud of what they have done so far, which may prompt them to do more. You might also want to remind them of something nice that they can do later, which encourages them to remember that it won't go on forever.

When your child is already really frustrated, you may find that these techniques don't work and that you need to try other tactics, but empathy is still an important part of addressing the problematic behaviour. You want your child to know that no matter how angry and hurt they feel, you are on their side and you empathise with them.

Tell them this, even when you are angry and upset yourself, because they will remember it and it's a good way to get through to them.

It is also important to offer empathy once your child has calmed down and got over their tantrum. Encourage your child to talk about how they have been feeling, why they behaved that way, and what you can both do differently in the future to avoid that sort of behaviour happening again. This is more likely to be effective with older children, but even young children can talk with surprising eloquence about how they feel, so don't miss the opportunity to ask your child what they are feeling, and to empathise with their emotions whenever possible. This sort of open communication will make it easier to talk your child down the next time they start a tantrum.

6) Prioritise And Pick Your Battles

You might be very keen to get started on the techniques that will help to improve your child's behaviour, but it's important to create a realistic plan and decide which areas you are going to focus on first, rather than launching into a huge wave of different tactics aimed at correcting all of your child's problematic behaviour at once. This will likely just result in you getting frustrated, your child getting frustrated, and a lot of alienation between the two of you. Even a small change may come as something of a shock to your child, and you need to give them time to adjust – so don't try to tackle everything at once, or you'll find you have a meltdown on your hands. Even if you make changes gradually, you're likely to get a lot of pushback at first, so make sure that you aren't overwhelming both yourself and your child.

Instead, identify a few key behaviours that you want to change. If your child does anything that endangers themselves or other people, these are the most important issues to address. For example, if your child is physically aggressive, focus on this behaviour before you work on something like table manners. Don't try to change everything overnight; your child will take time to adjust to your new techniques and the enforcement of rules, and you should take a gentle approach to minimise the trauma this causes on all sides.

You should also pick your battles, even once you have established your new techniques and your child is used to them. If your child is getting muddy but not hurting anyone, let them play, rather than dragging them inside to clean up. You will have more energy and patience for your parenting if you learn to let the little things go and just enjoy your child. If your child wants to tip toys all over the floor, let them – although it's fine to get them to help you when it's time to tidy up.

There is a fine balance between giving in (which you should not do) and picking your battles. A lot of this is about good communication with your child. You want your child to know that when you say something, it is firm and fixed. However, it is okay to decide in your own head that you are not going to start the fight. Think before you step in and tell your child to do something, and decide whether you really need to tell them to do it. If they are happy, quiet, and occupied, it's likely best to leave them.

7) If You Say Something, Mean It

It is often tempting to throw out empty threats when your child is being frustrating and upsetting, but you need to know that if you do this, your child will quickly learn that you don't mean what you say. There's then no reason for them to listen to you; they know that you will make threats that you don't follow through on, and that they can behave however they choose without consequences. Similarly, if you make empty promises – saying that your child can do X as a reward for completing Y – and then fail to make that happen, they will learn that you don't mean that either. Both punishments and rewards will lose their effectiveness and you will find that your child is extremely difficult to reason with and unimpressed by consequences even when they really matter (for example, in school) because they have the impression that consequences are not real.

You therefore really need to mean what you say. If you tell your child that they can only go out to play once they have picked up their toys, you need to follow that through. Similarly, if you tell your child that you want them to get into bed at 7 PM, don't let them keep pushing this later and later. You want them to respect the rules that you set and the things that you say. Make sure you follow up on both discipline and rewards, and don't let yourself or your child down by not meaning what you say.

This means that it's particularly important to keep away from setting unrealistic punishments. You need to make sure that the punishment is suited to the child's age, and remember that young children have very little concept of long-term punishments. There is no point in telling a 5 year old that they will lose their bike for a week if they don't behave; they will not differentiate this from losing their bike for an hour. You need discipline to be reasonably short, but effective, which is why many parents opt for the naughty step – this involves prompt but brief discipline that can then be forgotten about. It also gives the child an opportunity to calm down and prevents arguments from escalating. For older children and teenagers, longer punishments may be appropriate, but you should still aim for things that are realistic and that won't cause long-lasting resentment by dragging the discipline out.

You may find that it helps to have some standard punishments that you can turn to so that you don't get heated and come up with disciplines that you cannot follow through with. The naughty step is often the most effective go-to option for a young child, because it is immediate and can be enforced anywhere, but think carefully about what consequences you are happy to impose before you get into an altercation with your child. Use these, and don't be tempted to get creative when you are feeling heated by an argument.

All of these strategies are designed to help you take the tension and aggression out of your relationship with your child, and to make interactions easier. You may find that they are very difficult to employ to begin with, so make sure you are being patient with yourself. Don't get too angry if you make mistakes, but do apologise to your child. This can help to heal wounds that are inflicted when you argue, and there's a lot of power in apologising and owning a mistake. It will also show your child how they can come down from being wrong themselves, and sets a good example of honesty and openness.

The more you can employ these techniques in your everyday life, the smoother your relationship with your child should become. You can't expect miracles to happen overnight, but they should give you some of the tools that you need to succeed as a parent.

Create a Custom Behaviour Plan for Your Child

The above techniques are great, but one of the most effective ways of helping your child to behave well involves helping your child to understand how you want them to behave. Most kids, even those with O.D.D., are actually keen to please, even if they don't seem to be. You should therefore help them out by ensuring that they know what is expected of them and giving them clear instructions that they can refer back to at any time.

Your behaviour plan can be created in conjunction with healthcare professionals, but it may include elements such as:

- A routine
- A sticker chart
- A mood chart
- An outline of responsibilities
- Clear expectations
- A consequences list
- A parent's own guide for dealing with problematic behaviour

Let's look at each of these by turn and explore what they are and how they can help your child. Remember that the behaviour plan for your child is likely to change as the child grows, but that having a basic plan you can refer to may be invaluable. Your child's school may also opt to employ similar tactics, but may wish to work out a separate behavioural plan that is more optimised for learning in the classroom.

A Routine

We have already talked about scheduling, and this is going to be a key aspect of a behavioural plan. You should have an outline for your child's day and they should be able to look at this whenever they want guidance. If there are problem areas, you can then add more details about how you want the child to behave at those times.

For example, if your child tends to get restless and defiant at mealtimes, consider adding some instructions to the plan that tell the child how to behave instead.

Your plan might look something like this:

7:30 – Get up and get dressed.

8:00 – Eat breakfast. Sit at the table nicely and stay there until everybody has finished eating.

8:30 – Clear the table.

9:00 – Playtime with Sam. Remember to share toys and to ask when you want something.

A Sticker Chart

You are probably already familiar with the concept of a sticker chart, but these can be very effective for your child, especially when they are around 5 years old and up. They are a great option because they give the child a visual representation of the things that they are supposed to do, as well as a way to track their progress, and a reward when they reach a certain point. Most children love tracking things, and many love stickers, so a sticker chart brings together some key methods for encouraging your child to behave in particular ways. Sticker charts do need to be focused, however, so make sure you aren't listing a great swathe of tasks – choose some simple ones.

For a young child, you might have three or four columns, and these might says something like "Make my bed," "Put away my toys," "Do my homework." You should also make sure that the number of stickers that they need to earn is not excessive before a reward is offered. Even a small reward is usually sufficient for a child, so aim for every 10 stickers or so.

An older child may be able to manage a few more areas, but again, the sticker chart shouldn't be excessively long. Aim for concrete goals so that there's no argument over whether or not the sticker has been earned. You may find that it helps to have the child choose and put the sticker on personally; this can increase the engagement.

You can also use sticker charts to avoid negative behaviour, but as mentioned above, you may find it best to use positive language. For example, "Play nicely with friends" is a better option than "No hitting." However, to specifically curb aggressive behaviour, you may find that "no hitting" is effective.

A Mood Chart

A mood chart isn't necessarily part of a behavioural plan, but it can help you to create more communication with your child, and this will enhance other parts of the plan. Depending on how old your child is and how well they communicate, you might want to use smiley face emoticons. You can use Velcro to attach these to a chart so that your child can add an emotion to show you how they are feeling for the day, or allow them to draw a tick under the face that they are feeling.

This encourages your child to recognise their own emotions and deal with them effectively, and can help to prompt conversation. It also gives you insight into your child's feelings so that you are more likely to notice if their mood is consistently low, and find out what's wrong. This makes it easier to step in and solve problems before they get out of hand.

You can use the mood chart to prompt discussions with your child about how their day has gone and how they are feeling. This open flow of communication will make it much easier to relate to your child overall.

Outline Of Responsibilities

One of the things that you might struggle with is trusting your child to do things on their own, especially if they often misbehave when left unsupervised. However, trusting your child is a big aspect of making sure that they develop the tools they will need in life, and you can create a healthy relationship with responsibility by giving them tasks to do from an early age. These tasks should be rewarding for the child, accompanied by praise, and not too challenging. Think carefully about your child's abilities before setting tasks, and choose ones that they will be able to do, so they can feel proud of their achievements.

For example, you could encourage a child to set the table, putting out the right number of knives and forks for each person. You could also make your child responsible for filling water glasses (if they are old enough) or carrying plates into the kitchen after dinner. Other options include getting your child to do some easy weeding in the garden, asking them to put their toys away, encouraging them to dust, or requesting that they tidy up a small space such as a bookshelf, cupboard, or shoe rack.

While your child is doing this, let them figure it out, but be prepared to step in if they get stuck and want your assistance. It's important to give them ownership of the task so that they feel proud of what they have achieved afterwards, rather than getting frustrated by your intervention and wanting to give up because they can't do it well enough on their own. You should only intervene if you are asked for help or if your child is struggling and getting discouraged – and even then, encourage them to do what they can and to try things for themselves.

It's important to choose tasks that can be completed fairly quickly so your child doesn't feel a sense of dread. If you want them to get involved with bigger chores, try to break these down. You might ask them to sort the socks, rather than a whole basket of laundry, or tidy up one corner of their bedroom, rather than the whole thing. This is particularly important for children who suffer from O.D.D. and other conditions, such as ADHD. If they lose their focus and get bored before the task is complete, they won't feel the satisfaction afterwards, and it may result in frustration on both sides.

The outline of responsibilities can be stretched to other areas too, and it's a good technique to employ to ensure that your child understands what is expected of them and how they can undertake this. Teachers may use it in the classroom.

For example, they may tell the child that it is their responsibility to do 5 questions before playtime, or that it is their responsibility to stand nicely while in the lunch queue.

Creating expectations and following them up with rewards when they are met will teach the child accountability and make them more interested in doing the activity well than fighting the authority figure that has set the activity. Encourage your child to take responsibility for their toys, their meals, their appearance, and their time-keeping, and they are more likely to learn good life skills and do these things habitually, without being constantly nagged about them.

Set Clear Expectations

This is a key part of your behavioural plan; your child needs clear expectations. This is particularly critical if your child is on the autistic spectrum or suffers from any learning disabilities. An instruction that seems clear to you may not seem at all clear to your child, and this can lead to an immediate negative response, especially if you act frustrated when the child doesn't follow your instructions.

For example, if you tell your child to "set the table," your child may not know what to do, and this may result in a sense of panic or fear that leads to defiance and a refusal to complete the task. If instead you tell your child to "put 6 knives and 6 forks on the table," you offer the child a simple instruction that they can follow with ease.

This makes it much simpler for your child to do as you ask, so your behavioural plan should be built around these clear expectations.

The below examples may help to give you an idea:

- **Set the table:** put a knife and a fork next to every place, and then put a glass by every place. Put plates on the table.

- **Tidy up toys:** put each toy back in the box neatly, without throwing them. When the box is full, close the lid.

- **Tidy up after dinner:** carefully put the plates in a pile and carry them into the kitchen.

These can be adjusted to suit your child's age. Remember that the task should be quick and easy to complete, especially at first, so that your child gets a sense of satisfaction afterwards. You want to make it as easy as possible for them to obey you.

Consequences List

A consequences list does not need to be about punishment; it can have rewards on it too. The idea is to make sure that your child is clear about the expectations and the results of their behaviour. If they are going to get to choose a game for a family evening after they have tidied up their toys 5 times, they should know this. Similarly, if they are going to get their favourite dessert or a choice of movie, they should know this. Being clear about how their desired behaviour will result in positive consequences is a great way to encourage them to do what you want.

You may also want to create some negative consequences so that your child is equally clear about what will happen if they misbehave. It is generally agreed that children with O.D.D. respond better to positive consequences, but there will be times when discipline is necessary. You should have some punishments that your child knows will be imposed if they behave in a certain way. For example, you may send them to their room if they hit somebody.

It's important to remember that negative consequences are not particularly valuable with many children, especially those with O.D.D.

Almost invariably, experts have found that children respond better to positive rewards and goal-setting, rather than negativity and discipline.

Parental Guide

The parental guide is part of the behaviour plan that you might never want to share with your child. It is the part that reminds you of the things to do and not do with your child, and it's an important list to refer to as you grow and develop as a parent. It will remind you to do things like praise your child, encourage them, and listen to them. It will also remind you not to get into an argument with your child, and to use things like the Broken Record technique (where you repeatedly say something like, "I understand how you feel, but you must do X anyway") even when your child is being very frustrating.

You can develop this guide as you begin to establish new techniques, and learn the things that work with your individual child. Write out reminders to yourself, highlight tactics that work well, and generally create a bible of behaviour that helps you manage the difficulties you will face. You can also make notes about your child as they grow and change, which will help you when talking to medical professionals and determining what is effective and what isn't.

The Psychology of Child's Defiance and How to Deal with it in a Quick and Efficient Manner

An important part of dealing with O.D.D. is understanding it and recognising what causes it. This will put you in a much better position to manage it. What is the psychology behind O.D.D.?

It isn't known what prompts children with O.D.D. to behave as they do, but it has been closely linked with having a poor relationship with their caregiver(s), or being neglected or abused. It can also occur if discipline is inconsistent (and therefore not worthy of respect), as a result of a chaotic environment, or due to poverty. As it is also often linked with ADHD and autism, there may be other psychological causes. It can sometimes be connected with other mental conditions, such as bipolar disorder, language disorders, anxiety disorders, and depression.

It is important to note that children who suffer from O.D.D. do not think that they are being unreasonable. They see their behaviour as rational and logical, and merely a response to the unreasonable demands of others.

They may therefore get very set upon that response, and the more you try to argue with them, the harder they will push for it. A child with O.D.D. does not usually understand that they are being unfair, hurtful, irrational, defiant, or upsetting; they see themselves as behaving correctly, and the rest of the world as having wronged them. Remembering this may really help you to deal with your child, because it puts you in a better position to understand them. What seems a reasonable request to you may seem an unreasonable request to your child. Imagine if somebody came up to you and demanded that you give them your parking space. You would probably feel annoyed and indignant, and you would likely refuse. Similarly, if you were told you had to get off the computer and go to bed before you were ready, you might feel put out and irritated with the speaker. This is much what your child experiences when they are told to do something. Although there is a difference in that they are children and so have to obey the rules, they don't necessarily recognise that difference. They feel the same degree of indignation and "why should I?" about being told to do something that many adults would feel about being told to do something by someone with no authority over them. Understanding this may make it a lot easier to empathise when your child is refusing to do something completely rational and important; they don't feel that it is rational or important.

You may find it helps you to take a TACT approach to your child with O.D.D. This stands for:

- Triggers: recognising what upsets you and what upsets your child so you can work with these things, not against them.

- Acceptance: recognising that your child does not mean to be defiant; it is part of how their brain operates, and getting angry will not change this.

- Calming: find strategies that help you to get calm, such as stepping outside for some air or taking a few sips of water so you aren't lashing out when you are frustrated.

- Transitions: give your child time to switch their brain off one activity and onto another, rather than expecting them to snap from one thing to the other.

Give warnings about the transition and let your child take a break if necessary. This is particularly important for children with O.D.D. who also have ADHD, as it takes their brains time to swap.

Let's also cover one of the most effective techniques for dealing with O.D.D. in a quick and efficient manner: the Broken Record. We mentioned this in the previous chapter, but we'll look at it in more detail here. The Broken Record technique involves repeating your instruction kindly, calmly, and patiently, over and over again, until the child obeys. This may not sound like it should be very effective, but one of the great things it does is prevent you from getting drawn into an argument with your child.

A characteristic of O.D.D. is arguing, and you will likely find that when you ask your child to do something, you end up in a half hour discussion about why they should do it, with them finding more and more reasons that they don't need to, and ignoring your logical explanations of why they should.

For example, if you ask your child to get into bed, they may state that they aren't tired, and ask why they should go to bed when they aren't tired. This can easily devolve into an argument about their behaviour, how they get when they are overtired, statements about school or other commitments, and more – and it causes both parties to get frustrated and angry with each other.

Instead, you should show compassion for your child, but refuse to enter into a debate with them. You might say "I understand that you aren't tired, but you need to get into bed now anyway." You can say this calmly, without getting frustrated by the constant arguments that you won't win (as it's almost impossible to convince a child with O.D.D. through logic). You can say it as many times as you need to without escalating the situation.

This means you won't be feeding into your child's desire to get negative attention by riling you. If you start arguing with them, the child becomes invested in "winning" to prove that they are right and you are wrong, and they get your attention, your frustration, and the negativity that they are often seeking to create due to the disorder.

If you refuse to engage in the argument, you can shut it down and avoid either evoking the need to "win" or satisfying the need for negativity.

Another important aspect of shutting down the defiance quickly is to give yourself mental resilience, and you can do this by focusing on self-care. It is not selfish to do this. Parenting a child with O.D.D. is ineffably challenging and tiring, and allowing yourself to recoup will make you a much better parent overall. There are two aspects to this: giving yourself time and recognising when you need to walk away for a few minutes. Let's look at both.

Firstly, giving yourself time: you need to carve out some time to relax. Make some space in each day – even if it is only 5 to 10 minutes – in which you sit somewhere quiet and take the time to do something that you enjoy. This might involve having an uninterrupted cup of coffee, reading a few pages of a book, or just unwinding to some music.

It's very common for parents to feel guilty about this sort of behaviour, but you should remind yourself constantly that looking after yourself makes you a better parent.

You cannot be a good parent if you are worn down and exhausted. Next, you need to recognise when a situation is doing more harm than good and walk away from it. If your child has been screaming for 20 minutes and isn't listening to a word you say, take a deep, slow breath, and give yourself permission to disengage. If it's possible in the context, physically remove yourself from the space for a few minutes and do something different. This space will help your brain to reset and make it much easier to deal with the child. You should also work on something called a delayed response. It's very easy to get heated when you're dealing with a child who suffers from O.D.D. You are likely to feel angry and hurt by their behaviour, and this will prompt you to lash out and say things that you will later regret. You certainly are not alone in this, but the more you can put a stop to it, the better. The most effective way to do this is to make a conscious effort to delay your responses and think about your words.

This will give you a lot more control over what you say, and even – to some degree – how you feel. You need to be the calm one in the argument, so take the time to get there.

Not answering immediately may also help to calm your child down in some instances, because it will give them more space to think and may make them feel less "attacked" than if you snap back at everything they say. Try implementing a count to 5 before you answer something your child says in anger.

You should also try to learn your child's patterns and what sets them off, so you can mitigate these where possible. If, for example, your child particularly resents a direct instruction and prefers to be given some choice, you can work with this information and try to reduce those particular triggers.

Another great option is to find a neutral world that you and your child can communicate with when you don't want more negativity in the conversation, but you need a cue to stop. Some people use a positive word like "bubble" or "strawberry." This word can be a sign from you to your child that they need to take a deep breath and calm down. It can also be a word from the child to you to show that they are getting upset. It takes some of the negativity out of the conversation and can make it easier to communicate.

Positivity is an excellent tool to use when dealing with a child with O.D.D. The more positive and enjoyable you can make a situation, the more likely the child is to respond well to it and do what you ask. If instructions are always given in a negative tone, expecting a fight, you are more likely to get a fight. It's therefore important to be conscious of how you are approaching things and make sure you aren't being unnecessarily negative, even if this is hard at times.

Dangers and Mistakes You Must Avoid

We've covered some of the things that will help you work well with your child, but let's also look at some of the mistakes that you might find yourself making and how you can avoid these. You will find that if you stop doing certain things, your relationship with your child improves and you have an easier time with them. With that in mind, let's look at some of the top mistakes and danger areas to avoid.

1) Avoid Arguments

One of the first things to do is to avoid getting drawn into an argument with your child. You might feel as though you need to rationally explain something in order to get your child on your side when you are having difficulties, but actually, it's really important not to do this.

Debates about why something must be done will rarely work with a child, because they don't comprehend time in the same way as adults, and they have different priority lists.

A lot of children don't care about "later" because they live in the moment, so what they are interested in is the now. That means that explaining to your child that they must do their homework because they will need an education for their adult life will have little impact. Children simply don't reason this way. That isn't to say that children are stupid or incapable of reasoning – it's just that most children see this sort of thing in a different light.

This is true of many aspects of life. If you say to your child that they must go to bed now so that they aren't tired later, they won't really understand it, because they haven't developed their causality reasoning yet. Even a teenager may not have a fully developed sense of causality, although you are a lot more likely to be able to rationalise with a teenager than a young child.

Arguing is almost always a mistake. You aren't going to make your child suddenly see that you are being fair and practical with your instructions, and you are likely to increase your child's unwillingness to do whatever you are asking the longer you let the argument go on for.

If you don't take control and stop the argument from escalating before it has started, you'll soon find that both you and your child are frustrated, unable to find a middle ground, and getting angrier and angrier with each other.

2) Avoid Punishments

We have already talked about how negativity doesn't have a good effect on children with O.D.D., and in general, most experts agree that it's better to find rewards than to find punishments. You should have a go-to list of rewards that you can use, and a clear system whereby your child knows that they can do X when they complete Y.

For example, if your child asks to go to the park, you might tell them that they can do so once they have completed their homework. Here, the child is earning the reward, and the focus is on the positive and the potential for the future. They are more likely to feel that you are working with them and feeling proud of them than if you take something away. So, instead of telling your child that they will lose TV time if they don't set the table, offer them more TV time. They will see the potential to gain something they want and feel that you are making a fair exchange with them, and they are much more likely to complete the task. You have probably seen examples of this in your own life. At work, most companies reward employees as a means of encouraging exceptional behaviour, rather than punishing them for bad behaviour. Workplaces do of course have consequence systems, but you may be able to see how much more positivity and willingness are evoked by a rewards system, rather than a punishment system. The carrot usually wins above the stick, and it will certainly do so with a child who suffers from O.D.D.

Having some standard rewards that you can offer, based on the things that your child cares about, may help you to implement this system. Try to avoid using food as a reward, as this can cause unhealthy eating habits. Instead, reward your child with activities, stickers, movie choices, books, and more.

Note that it's very important not to "reward" your child by letting them not do what you originally asked of them. That task, whatever it is, should still be fully completed. If you have asked your child to tidy their room before watching TV, the reward for starting shouldn't be to only tidy half and leave the other half. You need to make sure that you are still getting what you require from your child, and not giving up. If you do, you will tempt them to push for you to give up again and again in the future, and it will become a lot harder to manage them at any time. Rewards should be separate from the activity you are asking them to do, so that there is no confusion.

Focusing on rewards doesn't mean that your child should never suffer consequences for their behaviour, but these need to be clear consequences, set when you are calm and level-headed. If you don't manage this properly, you will find that your child resents you and you make unrealistic threats.

3) Avoid Being At Odds With Other Caregivers

It can be hard to present a united front when you are dealing with a little one who is demanding, out of control, and frustrating, but the more you can get on the same page with other caregivers, the more effective your techniques will be. If your child knows that you will cave but your partner will not, they will turn to you instead of your partner when they want something and you won't be able to gain control of their behaviour. If they know that their teachers won't put up with misbehaviour but you will let them get away with it, you'll see them at their worst whenever they are at home.

This will also result in an overall lack of headway with your child, because inconsistency will often make them behave worse. If your child gets different responses from different people, they are more likely to keep testing the boundaries and pushing for responses so they can try to make sense of what they are seeing. Your child will be confused about how things work, and confusion is the enemy of a calm child. It leads to doubt, frustration, and a sense of mistrust for adults. If your partner sends one message and you send another, your child won't know what to think or how to deal with this. You need to find unity.

This often means agreeing upon strategies in advance, and then sticking to them even when this is difficult. You owe it to yourself and your partner – and other caregivers – to give your child this consistency and stability. If you disagree over how to handle something, consult with your medical professional or do some reading around the subject and come to a compromise, but don't teach your child that one parent will cave while the other will stay firm, or this causes resentment and frustration on all sides.

How to Build Your Child's Self-Esteem

It may surprise you, but a lot of children who suffer from O.D.D. also seriously lack self-esteem. Defiance is often a reflection of the fact that your child feels they are being attacked and the rest of the world is not being reasonable toward them. This is very likely to result in low self-esteem, and your child may often feel that things are their fault, even when they are lashing out and blaming the rest of the world. You should make yourself aware of this. Remember when your child uses harsh language and is aggressive towards you, it's because they feel bad about themselves and they are trying to find an outlet for that negative energy. Being positive and loving towards your child can go a long way to overcoming some of these issues, and building a bond between both of you that will make outbursts and aggression less likely. Children with O.D.D. are particularly likely to suffer from low self-esteem if they have other issues that make them feel "weird" or singled out from their peers. ADHD, autism, or learning difficulties can all destroy the child's confidence and self-belief.

With that in mind, let's look at some strategies for building your child's self-esteem.

1) Compliments

We all love to be complimented, but specific compliments are the ones that have the most power. Your child doesn't want a vague "well done," and this isn't very useful to them anyway. They need to hear why they did something well, so they know how to repeat the behaviour in future. You might say something like, "you shared your toys very well this morning," or "I am very proud of how hard you have been working on your writing." Make sure you reward effort, rather than achievements. It doesn't matter whether something was really done well or not; what matters is that your child tried. Competence will come with practice.

You should talk to your child's teacher about this too, and discuss how they can ensure your child feels like a success in the classroom as well as at home. You want your child to be proud and confident, as this will feed into their schoolwork and massively improve it. Discuss strategies for praise and encouragement, and also find out what areas your child might need more help with so you can provide this. Pay particular attention to praising your child for their work in these areas, because it's hard to feel enthusiastic about something if you think you're bad at it – and praise will address this problem.

2) Build Social Skills

A lot of children who suffer from O.D.D. struggle to create good relationships with their peers, and this have a massive impact on their sense of self-esteem. They will get left out of parties and events, and may start to feel isolated. This needs to be avoided at all costs. You should observe how your child interacts with other children and what problems they are running into when socialising so you can help them work on these problems. Skills like sharing and being empathetic need to be practised, so focus on providing your child with these skills. You can set up scenarios in which you show your child how good sharing feels, and encourage them to share with you, and then gradually expand this skill to their peers.

You may want to get input from their teachers on how they interact at school so you can further tailor your strategy. Set your child up for success by choosing smaller groups so they can feel comfortable and not left out, and find activities that they can enjoy. Praise your child for sharing, show them how proud you are, and encourage them to be as kind as possible. Remember too that your child will emulate the behaviour they see from you, so try to show examples of sharing in your daily life. For example, ask your partner if they would like a cup of tea, lend your gloves to them, "share" toys with your child. All of these things will help them to learn, which will give them better social skills and a better chance of forming strong friendships – and this will build up their self-esteem.

3) Be Affectionate

It isn't always easy to be affectionate when your child is stressing you out, screaming, angry, hurtful, or even violent. You might feel like it's really hard to love them, and even harder to show it. A lot of parents then feel guilty about this, which can make it even harder to show affection. Remember, however, that children need their parents to show them affection.

You should tell your child every day that you love them and that they are special. You can do this at bedtime as part of a routine. Don't refuse to do it because you are upset or angry with your child's behaviour; nothing they do should prompt you to withdraw your love or make them feel unwanted. If your child is to have good self-esteem, they need to know that you will always love them. You can explain that you don't love certain actions, but make it clear that you do love them without reserve.

Teaching Your Child Skills for Everyday Life

One of the most important things that you will do as a parent is teaching your child life skills that they will use each day, and while we touched on this briefly in the last chapter with building social skills, it's worth looking at it in more detail here. Some of these things are likely to be done in conjunction with the child's teachers, but here are a few that might help you.

1) Teach Them To Take Care Of Their Things

Many children who suffer from O.D.D. are prone to breaking things when they are angry, and there may be a temptation as a parent to replace those things when they get broken, just to forestall the tantrum. However, you should not do this.

If you simply buy toys whenever your child breaks them, your child will learn that there is no consequence to breaking those toys – and this is not a good lesson to teach, because it isn't true and it will hurt them in later life. They need to learn to look after their things, treat them with respect, and not expect immediate replacements if they damage things.

This will likely result in tears and tantrums when they discover they have damaged something that they love, but it's a crucial learning opportunity that may remind them to check their temper next time they are upset. You should also make sure that if they break something belonging to someone else, they lose (at least some) pocket money to pay for it, or have to offer something else up in return. This will help your child to establish that lashing out and damaging things has consequences.

2) Encourage Exercise

Exercise is not a blanket solution to the problems that your child will face, and it won't help them overcome every difficulty that they have in terms of their behaviour, but giving them an outlet can help considerably. Your child is more likely to feel good about themselves and the world if they are physically fit and healthy, and much more likely to be calm if they have a way to expend excess energy.

Sports can also really help your child to learn other valuable skills, like teamwork, cooperation, losing gracefully, and more. Participating in activities may help to expand your child's social circle and ensure they are making friends outside of school. Many children who have trouble focusing in the classroom can be good at physical activities. Of course, there are many challenges that your child may face, especially if they struggle with hand-eye coordination or other physical issues.

You should try a variety of sports to find one that your child enjoys and is good at. There are so many options out there, but you should look for something that your child loves. If possible, it's also a good idea to choose sports that involve social skills, such as cooperation, but any form of exercise can be beneficial.

3) Teach Your Child To Avoid Negativity

One thing that many children with O.D.D. fall prey to is negative cycles, and this can be a real problem when your child is trying to socialise, especially if they have siblings to deal with.

A child with O.D.D. will often struggle to ignore teasing from siblings, as they tend to have a very low tolerance and will get frustrated quickly.

Unfortunately, this can make them all the more fun to tease, since teasing is often about eliciting a reaction, and your child may get picked on as a consequence. If you have several children, you may find that they gang up on your child with O.D.D. because they can get a response.

You should therefore teach your child with O.D.D. how to avoid negativity (you may also want to teach your other children this, as it's a useful life skill, but we'll focus on teaching a child with O.D.D.). You should talk to your child about boundaries, both physical and mental. Your child should be told that they have a right to their own space, and that their siblings (and other children and adults) need to respect this space when asked. Teach your child how to ask for their space, and to state clearly when they want to be left alone. You should also talk to all of your children about respecting such statements, and fetching you if necessary when an argument can't be resolved.

Talk to your children about the fact that they have a right to walk away when someone is being negative towards them, and not to follow when someone exercises this right to walk away. Teach them to respect each other's bedrooms by encouraging them to knock and ask to be invited in. You probably won't get positive responses 100 per cent of the time, but keep encouraging this behaviour and ask your children to respect each others' spaces and right to be left alone. This should help to reduce fighting.

4) Teach Fairness

Fairness is a challenge for any parent, but it's very important if you have a child with O.D.D. Many children with O.D.D. have a strong sense of fairness when it comes to their own things, but not when it comes to others. That means you have to be firm about treating each other correctly. Be scrupulous about turn-taking, even with things that seem petty to you (like who sits where at dinner). This ensures that your O.D.D. child learns that they are not the centre of the universe, and your other children feel you are being fair. It may mean enduring tantrums from your child with O.D.D., but it's important to do this, or you are being ruled by your fear of the child, and they will soon learn that this is the case – prompting them to scream louder, kick harder, and generally behave even worse, because it gets them what they want.

Create visual, written rotas for the disputed points in your household and make sure that each child is being treated correctly. You should also encourage them to come and tell you if they feel that something is unfair, and weigh it up. If it isn't unfair, explain to them why, and if it is unfair, make efforts to correct it. This may not be perfect, but balance the scales as much as you can, as often as you can.

How to Help Your Child with Friendships and Socialising

Friendships and socialising, as mentioned earlier, can be very difficult for a child with O.D.D. They are not usually good at recognising the needs of others, and they often feel that you are against them when you are being fair. You may observe that your child with O.D.D. always wants it to be their turn, even when they have had multiple turns. It can be tempting to give in every time to keep the peace, but in doing so, you aren't making your child likeable and you aren't showing them how to behave. Unfortunately, this can lead to your child feeling exceptionally lonely and – if this issue isn't corrected – will cause long-term problems throughout the child's life.

Fortunately, there are things that you can do to help your child build some social skills. You may need to be their "practice buddy," but the time invested will pay back massively as you get to watch your child interact with friends in much healthier and more productive ways.

If you don't do this, you are likely to find that your child becomes steadily more isolated, and the more they get isolated, the more they will behave in outrageous ways.

Many of the social skills that other children pick up implicitly will be missing for your child, so you might have to take the time to explain them more thoroughly. You should view yourself as your child's emotions coach, and think about how you can explain the different aspects of play to your child. You should aim to cover things like:

- Being generous
- Sharing
- Being empathetic
- Being gentle with both words and physically
- Understanding cues
- Understanding expressions

Let's look at each of these by turn.

Generosity

You can work on this with your child by showing them how it feels when someone is generous towards them. If you have an older child, get them involved, or do this with your partner. Show your child how giving something that you want to somebody else and watching them enjoy it can feel good. Give them things that you have, and then encourage them to return the favour. This can enhance their understanding of why they might give something to somebody else, and may encourage them to do this with friends.

You can even go so far as to explain that people will like them more if they are kind and want to make them happy. This will help a lot with their understanding of the gesture. Don't be surprised or angry if your child struggles with the generosity element for a while, and don't punish them if they don't get it right. Instead, when they have an opportunity to be generous, verbally encourage them to be and praise them if they are. Remember too that your child doesn't need to be generous all of the time to be likeable.

Sharing

Sharing is a difficult one for all young children, and even as your child ages, they may struggle with it. Many children who suffer from O.D.D. also suffer from ADHD, and this may mean that they develop certain skills much later than other children of the same age. However, you should still work on this skill with them as much as possible.

Sharing can be worked on in lots of contexts, and should be made enjoyable wherever possible. Don't get angry if your child won't share, but gently prompt and encourage them whenever you see an opportunity to do so – and share with them in turn so that they can emulate your behaviour.

Being Empathetic

Teaching empathy can be very challenging, so it's something that you should work on with your child as much as possible. You may find that soft toys and storybooks are particularly effective ways to help with this. Encouraging your child to show empathy towards their toys, for example, may help them to grasp the concept without the social pressure. You might say that their toys are tired and encourage your child to put them to bed, or say that their toys are sad and encourage them to comfort the toy.

You can also encourage your child to empathise with family members, such as siblings, or pets. Talk to them about how they feel when they are hurt or sad, and show them how to relate these feelings to others so that they can show empathy.

Being Gentle

Teaching your child to be gentle is a good part of socialising, and you should focus on both words and actions. "No hitting" is a very important one for your child to learn early on, and one that you should work on as much as possible, especially if your child is prone to lashing out. This is one to work on with medical professionals if necessary, because it's really important. You can talk to your child about how being hit hurts and how dangerous it is – but if you're struggling, consider turning to the experts for help, because this is a critical social skill.

Words are also important to discuss. It is very common for children with O.D.D. to lash out verbally, saying things that are hurtful because they are frustrated and upset.

You may want to incorporate gentle language into the sticker chart or another rewards-based system so your child practices being kind. You should also work on this yourself – when frustrated, it's very easy to get harsh with your language. Avoid negative language, and avoid being critical. Instead, show your child how you can be nice with your words, even if you are upset about something. Remember that they will emulate your language, so if you lash out verbally when you are frustrated, they will do the same.

You could try writing out some positive and negative words on flashcards, and asking your child to help you pick the ones that are good to use, and set aside the ones that aren't. Form habits around positive language.

Understanding Cues And Expressions

You should also help your child get to grips with social cues and expressions. You may want to make some faces with exaggerated emotions on them and ask your child to identify these and explain what they mean to you, and how they should respond when they see these emotions. You should also talk about when to let someone walk away, how to respond to a negative phrase, and describe how to understand when someone is happy, angry, upset, etc., and what to do about these emotions.

This will help your child get to grips with some of the things that other children will pick up on more implicitly, and help to level the playing field so that they can interact better with their peers.

Breathing Techniques and Suggestions for Handling Intense Emotions

A child with O.D.D. often has intense emotions to grapple with, and you may need to help them develop coping strategies for these. This is particularly important if your child is physically destructive. Remember that they do this because they don't know how to deal with their emotions and it is too much for them to handle. You shouldn't punish your child for intense emotions. Instead, teach them to respect but manage their emotions, and help them find techniques that work for them. Techniques that will help them to feel calmer are key for so many situations in life that this is one of the most valuable skills you can pass on – so how do you do it?

Create A Calm-Down Space

This is a fundamental part of helping a child with O.D.D., especially if they suffer from certain other issues as well. Have an area that your child can retreat to when they need some space. This may be their bedroom, a quiet area of the living room, or another space, but it should be theirs and it should be respected.

It's not a space for playing or screaming in; it's a space for calming down.

You may wish to include sensory bottles or other toys that they can use for calmness, but there shouldn't be anything noisy, energetic, or disruptive. Consider some mood lights or other things that your child can look at and appreciate.

You might want to let your child calm down in this space alone, or sit with them. Make sure that it doesn't turn into an argument, and instead focus on encouraging some deep breathing or talking about how they are feeling. Use this as an opportunity to explain to them that you understand they are upset, and encourage them to stay in the space until they are calmer.

You may want to hold your child if they are calm enough to do so. You can put your arms around them or sit them on your lap. This kind of gentle pressure may help them to feel soothed and protected.

Having a safe space where your child can go to reset and giving them techniques that will help them when they are stressed empowers them to calm themselves when they need to, and will be a great life skill. You can use improvised spaces when you are out and about – such as a quiet aisle in a shop or something similar. Ask your school to set up a space for your child that they can retreat to when they need to.

Breathing Techniques

There are lots of breathing techniques that you can teach your child, and you should discuss these with the medical professionals and with your child so that you can find something that is effective. Different things will work for different children. Some of the techniques that you might want to try with your child include things like:

- **Square/Box Breathing:** Encourage your child to breathe in for 4 seconds and focus on how the breath feels, and then instruct them to hold their breath for 4 seconds. They should then slowly exhale through their mouth for 4 seconds, and then repeat these steps until they feel calmer.

- **Pursed Lip Breathing:** Get your child to relax their shoulders and neck, and then close their mouth. Tell them to inhale for 2 seconds, and then purse their lips and slowly blow out through their pursed lips for 4 seconds.

- **Lion's Breath:** Get your child to sit with their legs crossed and put their palms on their knees with their fingers spread out. They should then inhale deeply and open their eyes. Get them to stick their tongue out, as though trying to lick their chin, and create a "haaaa" sound as they breathe out. They should also try to look at the tip of their nose. This should be repeated around 3 times and is very good for creating a distraction.

- **Alternative Nostril Breathing:** Tell your child to gently close their right nostril with their thumb, and breathe out through the left nostril. They should breathe in through the left nostril, and then close the left nostril with their other fingers and release the right nostril to exhale. They can inhale through the right nostril, and swap back. This can be continued in a pattern until your child feels calmer.

- **Equal Breathing:** Ask your child to breathe in at a rate that feels comfortable to them, and then breathe out at the same rate. This could be 5 seconds in and 5 seconds out, or 8 seconds in and 8 seconds out, etc. Get them to keep up this equal breathing until they have calmed down.

While completing these breathing techniques, you should make sure that your child is sitting comfortably and in a place where they feel safe. They should be as calm as possible, away from distractions or the source of the upset.

The more you can practice these breathing techniques with your child, the easier they will find them to complete when they need to. Encourage your child to do deep breathing before bed, and possibly when they get up (depending on your morning routine and how much time there is). Get them to enjoy the comfort that the breathing exercises bring, and alternate if they find that their go-to one is losing its effectiveness.

Being disciplined about incorporating breathing techniques into everyday life — not just when your child is upset — will help to ensure that your child is good at these techniques and can perform them when necessary. They can then begin doing them on their own, either in their room or in another quiet space, whenever they need to. Try different techniques to find ones that work well. Some people find that a mood light that changes colour will help their child to regulate their breathing better.

Other stress techniques that may help your child include things like progressive muscle relaxation. For this, you should encourage your child to tense up a group of muscles, such as those in their feet, and hold them tense for about 5-10 seconds. They can then suddenly release the tension, and move on to the next muscle group. This can help them to remove tension from the body, and it may also feel good when they are really angry, because it will expend some energy when they tense up.

If your child is older and has a mobile phone, you may find that relaxation apps help them out. There are lots of free ones that may give your child more control over their emotions, and this will help them to feel more independent and in control.

You may want to implement a word that your child can give you that tells you when they need to calm down. This will help you to cut off a situation before they get hysterical, and gives them an easy out that they can turn to when they need it. Let them choose the word so they feel a connection with it.

You might also want to consider enrolling your child in a meditation class or a yoga class. Both of these things can give your child a better sense of self and the skills they need to relax, and they may also help them make new friends. Physical exercise is a great way to improve your mood, and yoga might be a good option if your child isn't in a position to enjoy regular sports (because they are too competitive, lack coordination, etc.).

Path to Outgrowing O.D.D.

Your child may outgrow O.D.D. if they are given the right support and techniques to overcome these issues. Around 70 per cent of children who suffer from O.D.D. do outgrow it, and this is particularly true of those who are given the right sort of help. However, many children who have suffered from O.D.D. will continue to experience some problems even as they enter adulthood. You should discuss this with your healthcare professionals and get assistance and advice on what to do and how to handle the transition. Many teenagers are particularly difficult to handle when they have O.D.D., so take advantage of as much support as possible at this time.

Unfortunately, many of the issues that O.D.D. causes will be a lot more serious when your child transitions into adulthood. Defiance, aggression, abusive language, and behaviour intended to irritate their co-workers will quickly cause problems at work, and your child may deliberately violate company policy just to see what happens. They may also really struggle to take criticism at annual reviews and meetings, and might not respect authority figures within the company.

Obviously, this will seriously limit your child's ability to enter the work world and learn to care for themselves and become independent. This can have a negative impact on their self-esteem and leave them feeling trapped, incompetent, and miserable. The faster you can get a handle on your child's behaviour, the more likely they are to be able to thrive in the work world and become an independent adult.

Outgrowing O.D.D. will not just happen automatically, and if it isn't treated correctly, it can develop into conduct disorder. Conduct disorder is associated with illegal behaviour, including stealing, drug abuse, arson, fighting, and more. If your child's lack of respect for authority figures continues, they may find that they get into serious trouble with the police, and face legal repercussions that have lifelong effects. It's very important not to just hope that your child will "grow out of" O.D.D., and instead to take active steps that will allow you to mitigate and overcome these problems. This will give your child their best chance of success in the fight against O.D.D.

To be clear, some children will outgrow O.D.D. before they

hit the age of 10, but many will not, especially if they continue to experience problems at home, or if they end up isolated, unable to make friends, and struggling with their schoolwork. You therefore need to take steps to tackle the problem as soon as your child gets their diagnosis. Remember that the more you invest energy in solving your child's problems while they are still young, the more likely they are to overcome their issues with defiance by the time they reach adulthood.

Don't depend on your child's age to solve the problems they are experiencing. Take real action to make changes to your child's life so that they can overcome their issues and turn into a functioning, happy member of society.

How to Monitor Child's Behaviour Progress and Improve it with Behaviour Mapping

Keeping a log of the things that your child does well and how their behaviour is changing over time can be a really powerful strategy in the fight against O.D.D. – because it shows both you and your child how much progress they are making. It's easy to feel like your strategies are ineffective and your techniques aren't working when you spend every day with your child, and you may find that you get discouraged or have a sense of stagnation, even when you are making progress. Because O.D.D. is such a frustrating condition to deal with, it's important to keep a record of your progress so you know that you are getting somewhere and your efforts are paying off. Don't neglect this.

You can monitor your child's progress in many different ways. You might find that it's effective to keep a diary that outlines when things are going well and what changes you're seeing, but one particularly effective option involves creating a behaviour map. You may want to start by outlining the behaviour that you think is particularly problematic so that you can see how it changes over time, and highlight for both yourself and your child when it is improving.

You might want both a negative and a positive behaviour map. A negative behaviour map might look something like this:

Date & Time	Action	Behaviour	Consequence
12/12/2012	[Sibling] took [child]'s game	[Child] hit [sibling]	Child sent for 10 minute time-out

By contrast, a positive behaviour map might look like this:

Date & Time	Action	Behaviour	Consequence
12/12/2012	[Sibling] asked for [child]'s toy	[Child] gave toy to sibling	[Child] was praised and given 10 minutes of TV time

You may also wish to add a column that says who observed the behaviour and set the consequence, especially if you are creating this behaviour map in conjunction with your child's school. Consider colour-coding the maps and involving the child in the process.

Over the period of a few months, you will find that this sort of mapping lets you see what areas are improving and how quickly, and also shows you what areas are lagging behind. If your child has stopped hitting but is still struggling with sharing, praise them for their progress but work more intensively with them on the concept of sharing. Choose games, movies, stories, and other things that encourage them to share. Show them how it's done. Keep mapping the behaviour, and you will hopefully see further progress in this area. Behaviour mapping can also be a really useful tool for others who are working with your child to see how they are progressing, and may help you to identify which techniques are working particularly well. If you're using a sticker chart to encourage your child to say nice things and your child's language use has massively improved, you might consider implementing the sticker chart in other areas.

Similarly, if you're finding that the promise of TV time is working particularly well to prompt sharing, keep doing this.

If a consequence or reward isn't effective, you're more likely to spot that it isn't working out through behaviour mapping, and you can then change your approach. You will therefore be far more effective at dealing with your child's O.D.D. and helping them to address the most challenging aspects of it.

You should bear in mind too that behaviour mapping lets you see how far you have come, and will give you a sense of pride and progress that can really help to motivate you when things seem hard. If you have a record that says 6 months ago, your child screamed whenever they were told to share, and now they are occasionally prepared to share, you can both be proud of this achievement.

It doesn't mean that the work is all complete and there's nothing left to do, but it does mean they have done well and they can be proud of it. You may even find that behaviour mapping is a great way to build your child's sense of self-esteem and encourage them to keep going — as well as encouraging yourself.

You can use other monitoring systems if they work better for you, but mapping like this is a great way to give yourself a lot of information about how you're progressing, what's effective, and how your child's behaviour is changing.

Conclusion

Raising a child with O.D.D. can be immensely challenging, and it's not something that you should try to struggle with alone. Get help and guidance from the professionals, and work in conjunction with your child's school to find strategies that work well with your child. Remember at all times that O.D.D. is not your child's fault, and that they need your help to overcome this challenge and become more functional. You are their guide in the world, and even when it's difficult, you have to be there for them. Remember that no matter how much you struggle with your child's behaviour, you must show them love, affection, and understanding.

A lot of dealing with a child who has O.D.D. involves patience and self-control. If you let your child wind you up, both parties will get upset, frustrated, and resentful. As the parent, your behaviour will have a lot of influence on how your child behaves, and the more you show them that they can rile you up and cause you to give in, the more they will push these boundaries, until you are ruled by the fear of upsetting them. Instead, you need to use your parental authority to set clear rules, offer rewards and impose consequences, and make sure that you handle your child as fairly as possible. This will create the guidelines a child needs to start trusting the world again.

Hopefully, you will have found the ideas and suggestions raised in this book helpful to you, and I'd like to leave you with some words of encouragement. No matter how hard it seems to be to make any headway, you are making an effort – just by reading this book. You are investing in your child's future, you are trying to make things better for them, and you should have faith in your own ability to do this. You don't have to be a perfect parent in order to overcome some of the difficulties that your child faces with O.D.D. Be kind to yourself, give yourself some space when you need it, and remember that you are trying. Don't beat yourself up when you don't handle a situation as well as you meant to. Instead, analyse what went wrong, how you can make sure it goes better next time, and go forward from there.

---

i   Access NCBI through the World Wide Web (WWW). (1995). *Molecular Biotechnology*, *3*(1), 75. https://doi.org/10.1007/bf02821338

Printed in Great Britain
by Amazon